Boston

BOSTON

Nancy Sirkis

INTRODUCTION BY
Edward M. Kennedy

A Studio Book
THE VIKING PRESS
New York

First published in 1966 by The Viking Press, Inc.
625 Madison Avenue, New York, N.Y. 10022

Published simultaneously in Canada by
The Macmillan Company of Canada Limited

Senator Kennedy's introduction and some of the pictures first
appeared in Esquire.

Library of Congress catalog card number: 66-16069
Printed in U.S.A.

Designed by Christopher Harris

Contents

INTRODUCTION:

My Boston

EDWARD M. KENNEDY

When I was six years old, and my grandfather, John F. Fitzgerald, was seventy-five, he used to take me around Boston and show me the historic places. I would meet him at the Bellevue Hotel, next to the State House. We would have lunch in the dining room, where all his political friends would stop at his table to say, "Good to see you, Honey Fitz," and he would introduce me, very solemnly. In the same way he would take me to the kitchen to meet the chef and his staff. After lunch, we would walk together down Park Street Church, where William Lloyd Garrison had preached against slavery, and then we would go to the Old South Meeting House, where the speeches of James Otis and Samuel Adams had fired the Revolution. Grampa would show me the place on the Common where British soldiers drilled, and where they had boarded the boats to cross the Charles River and begin the march on Lexington and Concord. We would wander over to Spring Lane, the site of a well from which Boston had drawn all its water for a great many years, and over to Beacon Hill, where he showed me the cobblestones of Louisburg Square, which, according to legend, had been used as ballast in ships that brought the immigrants.

We would go down to the harbor, with its rusting old wharves and trawlers, and its sea gulls feasting on discarded scraps of fish. He always said that Boston, not New York, should have been the great port of the East, since it was about two hundred miles closer to Europe than New York.

Grandpa had been Mayor in 1906 and 1907 and from 1910 to 1914. He had put the first Christmas tree on the Common, and built the first bandstand. He knew everything that went on in the city. "Have you heard that Mary O'Reilly has left to teach school in New York?" he would say. "We have to pay our teachers more." Or, "They haven't had squash pie at Hayes-Bickford's restaurant for three days. Can't we get the food to market faster?"

Grandpa was very fond of his city. His slogan was "A Bigger, Better, Busier Boston." To me he will always be the spirit of Boston.

Later on, with my brothers and on my own, I saw the other parts of Boston, which tourists rarely reach. Originally almost an island, little more than a mile square, Boston grew by scaling down its hills and using the earth to fill in the water. It is nothing you can tie together. It was never laid on a grid, or planned by a council. People built houses where they wished, and made paths to visit their neighbors. Out of these grew little streets, impossible to follow, which twist and narrow and end in flights of stairs. Every neighborhood is different. The tides of immigration have moved in and out. No one could ever say who would come next, or where they would settle, or what they would do.

The North End is a taste of southern Italy—crowded streets, alive with people, the smell of the bread shops and the open-air markets piled with fresh produce, cheeses, sausages, live snails and squid, enormous wedding cakes in the windows of the stores, groups of men on street corners arguing and playing mora. Its streets are tiny. My brothers and I used to play a game to see who could cross Hanover Street—the main street of the North End—in a hop, a skip, and a jump. The red-brick buildings are old, but inside they are clean and modern, and people tend gardens of orange trees and fig trees on the rooftops.

Charlestown, because it is on a hill and receives the sea breezes, is a very different place: open and airy, remote from the stress of the city, its life shaped by the triple-decker houses and men who work close to the sea. East Boston is even closer to the sea, its streets named after the great ports of the world—London, Havre, Paris—its houses fitted with widows' walks, where women kept watch for their men bound homeward in the fishing boats.

Beacon Hill is staid and proper, with streets named Joy and Pinckney and homes with lavender windowpanes. It is no longer the citadel of the Brahmin. Large apartments have been built at its foot, and many of the buildings with their tunnels and secret gardens have become apartments for young single people. But the tone of the hill is still set by the ladies who go to the symphony on Fridays, and to evenings of waltzes at the Sheraton Plaza Hotel.

South Boston, with its churches and wide beaches; Roxbury, with its brick row houses; Back Bay, with its libraries and museums and concert halls—Boston is all of them, with their different moods and different kinds of people.

Like a sponge in the sea, Boston is an accretion of small pieces of charm, deposited over a long period of time by people who cared. My wife can go to the Harvard Musical Association on Beacon Hill and play a piano free of charge, because ladies like Mrs. Lucy Marsh loved music and wanted people to have a chance to play. Mrs. John Lowell Gardner II had a place built in the Venetian manner, lived in it, filled it with art, of which some was selected by Bernard Berenson, and left it as a public museum.

Boston is a feeling—a sense of having learned long ago what it is that makes a city appealing. If the finest architects and landscapers and the best experts in modern living were asked to plan an ideal city, they would come up with much that Boston already has.

Like a river. Every great city should be on a river. It gives a feeling of space and sky, majestic by day, shimmering by night. Some cities have cut their people off from their rivers by expressways and such, but not Boston. Sailboats and sculling boats fill the waters of the Charles. Students study on its banks. I take my children to the Esplanade on the riverbank to hear concerts by the Boston Pops Orchestra. Last year, a proposal was made to cut down nineteen sycamore trees on the Cambridge side of the river. The nation's most famous public-relations man led a campaign of protest. Students threatened to chain themselves to the trunks. The plan never had a chance.

Or like a Common in the middle of the city, and a Public Garden. Not a small park, tucked away between skyscrapers, or a meager piece of green space in a new development where pathetic little trees are tied to wooden rods for safety—but seventy-two acres of the most valuable real estate in town, next to the busiest shops and the center of government. The Common gives every man in Boston an estate, a place to relax in the sun before plunging into the life of the city. In the spring, the Public Garden is full of flowers; in summer it is a lazy place where children ride on swan boats in a lagoon; at Christmas, the Common is a wonderland with lights and caroling and live animals in the manger.

Or a way of doing business that is graceful and unhurried. Boston is the mercantile center for almost ten million people, but men still work at standup desks and eat at restaurants with sawdust on the floor, and stop to visit with each other on the street. Some of them may take some extra time off at lunch to leaf through obscure magazines at the Athenaeum. The central office of one of the largest banks retains the wooden chairs and lanterns of an old countinghouse. It is still possible to have new heels put on men's shoes in the middle of the business district, while they wait, at lunchtime.

Bostonians like the feeling of being steeped in history. They give special deference to the old—the ancient buildings, the small shops, the restaurants with the large overhead fans where their grandfathers ate, the old characters who stand around the Court House. The bell ringers have been playing the same music from Louisburg Square since the turn of the century. No one will disturb these, because they are what makes Boston distinctive.

A nineteenth-century city, Boston has allowed the present to be imposed upon it without wincing. It realizes its responsibilities, as a center of medicine, culture, education, and scientific research. It knows it is a part of the wealthiest and most industrial area in the world, that its population will increase, as well as its importance, and with them will come the need for more skyscrapers, apartments—and expressways. Many parts of Boston that are shabby and devoid of history are coming down. The city *is* bigger, better, and busier—my grandfather would have been proud.

Yet something in the Boston spirit seems to say that, vital and progressive as all the new will be, it never will be Boston's personality. That always will be lodged somewhere among the small wharves and chimney pots; off a crooked little alley leading to a rare-book store; in among the men in old tweed coats who argue on the Common; in the glow of the lighted candles in Beacon Street windows on Christmas Eve; in the fog gathering off the harbor on a gray November day.

By its irreverent charm, Boston has enticed its people, generation after generation, to love it as it is, and they are not going to stop.

Preface

NANCY SIRKIS

My involvement with Boston started quite by accident. One day when we were working on another project, Bryan Holme, my editor at The Viking Press, casually remarked that Boston would be an excellent subject for a picture book. Although I was a total stranger to the city, the word "Boston" evoked so many historical and cultural contrasts—Paul Revere, Ralph Waldo Emerson, *The Late George Apley*; "The Hub of the Universe" and "The Athens of America"; Harvard and MIT; the late Mayor Curley and Irish politics; the Sacco-Vanzetti case; the Kennedy family—that I was immediately interested.

Boston more than lived up to my expectations. It is a kaleidoscope where past, present, and future constantly interweave. After almost half a century of stagnation, its citizens have recently taken an honest look in the mirror and become frightened at the sight of a dying metropolis. For a long time it was easier to think of the great cultural and historical past than to face up to the present, but now the city has begun moving into the twentieth century.

Today Boston displays all the effects of those years of neglect. The grandeur of the view across the Charles River from Cambridge is marred by a haphazard skyline, and the overhead expressways tear apart the city as if an earthquake had created chasms between buildings. Out of the quiet brick houses of Back Bay appear skyscrapers which have no visual relation to the older, low buildings, or to one another. But the urban-renewal program is dedicated to creating a beautiful new city that will coexist with the best of the old. And the city's personality, as expressed in the faces of its citizens, at once commanded my attention.

Unlike New York, Boston never became a "melting pot." Generations of inbreeding have given Yankee Bostonians an especially prim and austere look, and Irish Bostonians look especially boisterous and ebullient. The dominance of these two ethnic groups, and their diametric oppositeness in many aspects of character, background, and temperament, make Boston unique among large American cities.

I set out with my cameras to discover just how these two so different strains lived, and how the city of Boston worked. In doing so, I explored visually the Yankee-dominated banking, business, and cultural community, the largely Irish-controlled political scene, and the vast educational-scientific-industrial-medical complex.

For me, perhaps the most wonderful thing about Boston is that because its individual groups and worlds have not fused into one large urban mass, it retains much of the flavor of a small town. Walking from Beacon Hill, the last stronghold of the Yankee, with its elegant, quiet streets reflecting the wealth of a bygone era, through the business district, to the Italian North End and its crowded streets lined with sturdy brick buildings, is like crossing a national border. For although Boston's citizens are finally working together, they are not living together, and the cultural contrasts are sharp, the diverse traditions stubbornly maintained. Even new establishments, such as the "think" firms on Route 128, quickly manufacture their own sets of patterns and rituals.

For the reasons I have indicated, I found Boston's people a greater attraction than its rapidly changing architecture. And that is why this book, with all due respect to the city's topography, is intended primarily as an informal portrait of the people, politics, and the dreams comprising Boston today.

New York, 1965

ACKNOWLEDGMENTS

No book that pictures as many different people and places as this one could have been accomplished without a great deal of help.

I am especially indebted to Marion and Paul Fremont-Smith, who provided me with a home away from home, and whose advice and counsel appears in some form in every section of this book.

To my friend Don Young I am grateful for an introduction to "Southie" (South Boston) and to many politicians.

For sharing their insights into Boston politics, and for much guidance and practical help in understanding their native city, I am grateful to John Powers and Robert Quinn.

My introduction to and knowledge of Boston's North End were facilitated by Frank Harvey of the North End Union.

Roy McDonald, John Calkins, Gabriel Piemonte, Mr. and Mrs. Benjamin Ellis, and John P. Marquand, Jr., all helped me enormously in my quest for knowledge of different aspects of the city.

I am grateful to Cornell Capa for advice on the ruthless editing of photographs, to Charlotte Trowbridge Dyer for her advice on layout, to Joseph Portogallo for his superb prints.

Last, but most important of all, I wish to thank my husband, Frank Horch, without whose help, advice, and encouragement this book could not have been accomplished.

N. S.

I

The Yankees

T he descendants of the English settlers who founded Boston over three hundred years ago are a small minority in the city today. The Yankees lost effective
political control to the Irish early in the twentieth century. Their clipper ships and
textile mills, which brought wealth to Boston, have been replaced by technological
or "think" firms in the suburbs, staffed by outsiders of varying descent. Harvard
University, most of whose students once reflected the views of the Puritan Yankee
founders, is now representative of all groups and areas of the country. Most of the
"proper Bostonians" do not even live in Boston these days; they commute to it from
the suburbs. And yet, so pervasive has been their influence that the face, manner,
and feeling of this now predominantly Irish city are still Yankee.

The original settlers of Boston were Calvinist Puritans, more severe and conservative than the Pilgrims who had come earlier on the *Mayflower*. Religion was a
dominant force in the lives of these settlers; but, austere and godly as they were,
they were not necessarily modest. From the first, Bostonians were rather pleased
with their colony and themselves. As John Adams wrote of a later era: "The morals
of our people are much better; their manners are more polite and agreeable; they
are purer English; our language is better, our taste is better; our persons handsomer;
our spirit greater; our laws are wiser; our religion is superior; our education is
better."

Soon their incomes were better too. The lowly codfish proved such a source of
wealth that at one time well-to-do Bostonians were known as "the codfish aristocracy."
It was the cod that led the colonists first to build small fishing boats and then larger
ships for ocean trade. By 1774 Boston was a prosperous maritime community, and the
stage was set for the rise of the great merchants who were to found the family fortunes
that sustain many Yankee Bostonians to this day.

The stage was set also for the American Revolution, in which men whose descendants are still prominent in Boston came to the fore as leaders: John Adams, a
signer of the Declaration of Independence, became the first Vice-President and the
second President of the United States, and with his wife Abigail founded a line that
has included another President, three Ministers to England, several Cabinet mem-

bers, and a number of distinguished literary men, including the author of *The Education of Henry Adams*. The famous Revolutionary figure "Old Judge" John Lowell, grandson of Percival Lowle, who settled in Boston in 1639, filed more than seven hundred libels against British vessels captured by American privateers; the Massachusetts Bank he helped to found became the First National Bank of Boston and grew to be one of the largest in the country. One of the Old Judge's sons, Francis Cabot Lowell, introduced cotton manufacturing to America, thereby revolutionizing the New England textile industry; among the other Lowell descendants were churchmen, philanthropists, and educators, a noted astronomer, and a number of poets, including James Russell Lowell, Amy Lowell, and Robert Lowell of the present generation. In Boston, as the saying goes, the Lowells "talk to the Cabots, and the Cabots talk only to God." The Cabots began their rise to eminence with George Cabot, a Salem merchant and shipowner who was a powerful force in New England politics during and after the Revolution, and a strong supporter of the Federalists and Alexander Hamilton; latter-day Cabots, and Cabot Lodges, have tended to be of Republican political persuasion.

The general prosperity of the time, and a devotion on the part of leading Bostonians to public service and the pursuit of culture, combined to make the nineteenth century a true golden age for the city. If Boston was not "the hub of the universe," as its citizens claimed, it certainly was "the Athens of America"; there were more statesmen, educators, and literary figures gathered there in that period than in any other American city. The *Atlantic Monthly*, one of the more enduring monuments of Boston's literary pre-eminence, was founded there in 1857—born out of a luncheon conversation in which Ralph Waldo Emerson, Henry Wadsworth Longfellow, Oliver Wendell Holmes, and James Russell Lowell (who became the *Atlantic*'s first editor) took part. The magazine published such writers as Nathaniel Hawthorne, Henry David Thoreau, Mark Twain, Bret Harte, and has carried its high literary standards into the twentieth century. Boston has kept its Athenian atmosphere; Edward Weeks, editor of the *Atlantic* from 1938 to 1966, said recently of the city's continuing attraction for writers, "People with talent go where it is congenial to write, and it is congenial to write in Boston."

Another of Yankee Boston's cultural traditions that has carried over from the nineteenth century is the Athenaeum, a privately endowed library founded in 1807 that was a forerunner of the public library system, independent of any college, academy, or learned society. Under its present Director, the historian Walter Muir Whitehill, who is also chairman of the Boston Historical Conservation Committee and president of the New England Historical and Genealogical Society, the Athenaeum has continued to cater to the interest of its shareholders in the arts, philosophy, and history, and in cultural and historical preservation. Outsiders who wish to use the library must be "referred" by one of its shareholders.

The Boston Symphony, established in the 1880s, is another survivor of the city's golden age—a flourishing survivor despite its annual deficit, which Bostonians have always cheerfully made up out of their own pockets. Its complex affairs, including the raising of funds, are administered now by Henry Cabot, as president of the board of trustees. Running the Symphony "is like the measles; you have to be exposed to it to catch it. Only, unlike the measles, once you catch it, you enjoy it," says this epitome of all that is Yankee Boston.

Mr. Cabot is typical of a cultural pattern that obtains in Boston, pointed out by the historian Samuel Eliot Morison; when a family acquires great wealth, it does not continue to seek it, or build monuments to its name, but invests its energies and often its money in art, music, and literature. Families such as the Lowells, Eliots, and Cabots encouraged their younger members to go into financially unproductive fields, and the tradition of one son watching over the family business while the others devote their lives to public service, or scholarship, still persists.

Ralph Lowell, present head of the Boston branch of the family, combines the two aspects: known familiarly throughout the city as "Mr. Boston," he is not only chairman of the board of the Boston Safe Deposit and Trust Company, a life member of the M.I.T. Corporation, and honorary vice-president of the Boston Chamber of Commerce, but also president of the board of trustees of the Boston Museum of Fine Arts and a trustee of the Massachusetts General Hospital. At one time Mr. Lowell served simultaneously on the boards of no less than fifty-two organizations or institutions, educational, charitable, medical, financial, and cultural.

Not only are Yankee values of thrift, conservative behavior and dress, and shrewd business sense passed on from generation to generation in Boston; professions also are handed down. Dr. George Cheever Shattuck, for years Clinical Professor of Tropical Diseases at Harvard Medical School and the Harvard School of Public Health, is the fifth generation of his family to practice medicine, and the third Dr. Shattuck in a direct succession to be associated with the Harvard Medical School.

The nineteenth-century concept of public service deeply underlies the career of Henry Cabot Lodge, who, following in the footsteps of his grandfather (whose name he bears), has been United States Senator from Massachusetts, Ambassador to the United Nations, Ambassador to South Viet Nam, and a candidate for Vice-President in 1960 on the Republican ticket, and was in the running for Republican Presidential candidate in 1964. His son, George Cabot Lodge, is already well advanced in a similar career; he has been Director of Information for the United States Department of Labor and Assistant Secretary of Labor for International Affairs. Now teaching at the Harvard Business School, where he is director of the Central American project and Associate Director of International Activities, the younger Lodge has shared with his father the misfortune of running against a Kennedy in a political contest; he was defeated for United States Senator by Edward M. Kennedy in 1962, as Henry Cabot Lodge was defeated by John F. Kennedy for the same office in 1952—thus dramatizing the confrontation of Yankee Boston, of which the Lodges are superbly representative, with the Irish immigrant stock from which the Kennedys come.

On the distaff side, Yankee Bostonian women have always been noted for their independence, energy, public-spiritedness, and obliviousness to fashions and fads. Abigail Adams Homans, great-great-granddaughter of the first Abigail Adams, has devoted much of her life to charity work and was long the only woman on the board of the Massachusetts General Hospital. She says of today's Boston, "Everything is changed; the whole concept of life is different since I was a girl. Today all girls go to college. I wanted to go to college, but my mother's reaction was, 'Why? You're only young once.' So I was sent abroad to be finished." Now in her eighties, Mrs. Homans can be seen in the worst blizzards, in a heavy coat, knee-high galoshes, and sensible broad-brimmed hat, indomitably airing her dog, Minniehaha.

The Curtis sisters, Margaret and Harriot, also provide admirable examples of the female Bostonian's zeal for causes and for useful activity. Margaret Curtis, who died in 1965, was trained in social work after World War I and was active with the Red Cross and other agencies in aiding refugees in many parts of the world. Harriot Curtis, the elder of the two sisters, was for five years Dean of Women at Hampton Institute, an industrial school for Negroes in Virginia, and also worked for Children to Palestine, and to aid other minority groups. Both sisters displayed a lifelong passion for golf as well as good works; Margaret Curtis was National Women's Open Champion in 1906, 1911, and 1912, and Harriot in 1908.

Nor have Bostonian ladies abstained from political action when the situation required it. No one was faintly surprised when Mary Parkman Peabody recently spent a night in jail in St. Augustine, Florida, after taking part in a civil-rights demonstration. "That's the kind of thing she does," said her husband, Bishop Malcolm E. Peabody. "I've never tried to stop her." Nor did her son, Endicott Peabody, then Governor of Massachusetts, or her daughter, Marietta P. Tree, a member of the Human Rights Commission of the United Nations. Mrs. Peabody was merely performing a twentieth-century variation on the Yankee pattern of arriving at one's own convictions and proceeding to put them into effect. "I don't feel that a child can grow up in a segregated school and still feel part of the group," she said. "In going to jail, I was just doing what any American ought to be doing."

Twentieth-century concerns are having their effect on even the most securely entrenched of the Boston Yankee families. One Yankee Bostonian engaged in adapting the ways of his ancestors to modern life is Charles Francis Adams, "oldest son of an oldest son," the fourth Adams to bear that name and the fifth generation in direct descent from John and Abigail Adams; he is chairman of the board of Raytheon, Inc., an electronics firm that is the second largest employer in Massachusetts. For Bostonians such as George Peabody Gardner, Jr., an investment banker and chairman of the United Fruit Company, or Samuel Walcott, Jr., a private trustee who services —and helps to conserve—the fortunes of prominent fellow citizens, the banking scene in Boston, still one of the great financial centers of the United States, may have remained largely as it was for their Yankee ancestors. But Ephron Catlin, Jr., senior vice-president of the First National Bank of Boston and former president of the Boston Chamber of Commerce, finds a challenge in getting the city moving forward into a new era. Catlin, a Midwesterner and a Roman Catholic who came to Boston via Harvard and marriage to a Boston girl—a Saltonstall—has been a leader in inducing the banking community to accept and to finance the new electronics industry for which the city is becoming a center. "They all have to listen to me," he says, "for I'm half Yankee and half Irish, and therefore compatible with everyone." And Catlin, who believes seriously that Boston will not really "work" until Yankees and Irish finally do get together, has been influential in bringing such cooperation about.

Dr. George Cheever Shattuck

Margaret and Harriot Curtis

Mary Parkman Peabody

Charles Francis Adams

Edward Weeks

Walter Muir Whitehill

OVERLEAF: George and Henry Cabot Lodge

Ephron Catlin, Jr.

George Peabody Gardner, Jr.

Samuel Walcott, Jr.

Architecture

Boston's earliest settlers built their austere wooden dwellings in what is now the downtown district; fire was a constant threat, and the only remaining example of these seventeenth-century wooden houses is the one later lived in by Paul Revere, in the North End *(page 73)*. Brick came into use in the eighteenth century, and in Boston's Federal period—1775 to 1837—the free-standing wooden buildings gave way to rows of brick houses, often attached, lining the new, straight streets. Georgian England was the chief influence of the period, which was dominated by the work of Charles Bulfinch; the red brick center portion of the State House is probably his best known work.

The Greek Revival style, of which a number of the houses in Louisburg Square on Beacon Hill are examples, prevailed in the mid-nineteenth century, when Boston was becoming known as "the Athens of America." Also dating from the nineteenth century are the distinctive three-decker houses *(page 125)*—many of them displaying beautiful carvings on the doorways—in South Boston, Dorchester, Roxbury, and Charlestown, where the Irish immigrants lived and where many an Irish politician was born.

Almost no construction took place in the city in the first half of the twentieth century; then, in the 1950s, emerging from the long political stalemate between the Yankees and the Irish, Boston began racing to catch up with other cities, where steel and glass buildings were thrusting skyward. Her present appearance suggests a city devastated by war, with excavations, bulldozers, and scaffolding everywhere; but out of the rubble, in the Back Bay area, has arisen the fifty-two story Prudential Building, the highest in the United States outside of New York and Chicago, to dominate the skyline and serve as the visual symbol of "the new Boston."

OPPOSITE: Statue of Paul Revere, with the steeple of the Old North Church
PAGES 40-41: Beacon Hill houses overlooking Boston Common
PAGES 42-43: Old Granary Burying Ground; details from some gravestones
PAGE 44: Acorn Street, Beacon Hill
PAGE 45: Louisburg Square
PAGE 46: Copley Square, with Trinity Church in the foreground, the Boston Public Library, built by McKim, Mead and White, in the background
PAGE 47: The façade of Trinity Church, built in 1877 by H. H. Richardson
PAGE 48: Housefronts on Commonwealth Avenue
PAGE 49: Congress Street, in the heart of Boston's financial district

In Memory of

Culture

In Boston, culture often extends from being a merely private pursuit to the founding of institutions; notable among the latter are the Gardner Museum and the Boston Symphony. The Museum, a Venetian *palazzo* brought over in bits and pieces from Italy and re-erected in Boston's Fenway, was the home of Isabella Stewart Gardner, a New Yorker who came to Boston in 1860 as the wife of a wealthy Yankee, John Lowell Gardner. Mrs. Gardner's passion for Renaissance art was as extravagant as the styles of dress and behavior with which she shocked the ultra-conservative Bostonians, and after her husband's death she devoted herself to acquiring great works of art. Her *palazzo* and the treasures it housed were open to the public after 1903, though she continued to live there until her death in 1924. She designed a seal bearing a phoenix, symbol of immortality, with the phrase, *"C'est mon plaisir"* ("It is my pleasure") as a motto—and put this policy into effect by leaving funds in her will for the permanent maintenance of the collection in the palace of which, for her own pleasure, she had made a museum.

If for Mrs. Gardner the pursuit of art was a way of life, attending the Symphony has become that for hundreds of Bostonians. Founded in 1881 by Henry Lee Higginson, by its third season the Symphony had become so popular that there were long lines waiting to purchase tickets, and a subscription system had to be initiated. However, to further an ideal of providing good music at reasonable prices, two hundred tickets for the Friday afternoon concert have always been made available at a nominal price—currently 60 cents—at the box office the day of the concert. These unreserved seats go on sale at 1 p.m. each Friday, and the line of purchasers begins to form well before 9 a.m. The same faces *(pages 52-56)* appear in the line in approximately the same order each week, and often books, games, and even chairs are brought along to while away the hours of waiting. The Boston Symphony is unique in that it has only one conductor—at present Erich Leinsdorf *(page 57)*—and the longest season of any city symphony: forty-six to forty-seven weeks of the year, including an eight-week summer season at Tanglewood. Its Friday afternoon concerts are the high point of its thirty-three-week season in Boston.

The Isabella Stewart Gardner Museum

ABOVE and OVERLEAF: The Friday afternoon line at the Symphony

Music lovers waiting to hear Erich Leinsdorf—shown opposite at a rehearsal—conduct the Boston Symphony

Bostonians still take the waltz seriously; a Waltz Evening is held monthly during the season at the Sheraton Plaza (formerly the Copley Plaza) Hotel.

II

OPPOSITE: The Old North Church, whose steeple looks down on the chimney pots of Boston's North End, and across to tugboats on the river.

The Italians

The streets of the North End, the Italian section of Boston, are teeming with life at all hours of the day. On their way to market in the morning, black-shawled old women, hair pulled back in neat knots, stand gossiping with their neighbors in rapid Italian punctuated by gestures; when schools let out in the afternoon, shouting youngsters chase each other and their pets through the narrow byways; men congregate in front of the cafés in the evening, or play *boccie*. Over this vivid scene float delicious odors from the outdoor market stalls, from salamis and cheeses hung on great hooks in the store windows, from olives and freshly baked bread.

A city within a city, the North End is cut off physically from the rest of Boston by the waterfront on one side and an elevated highway on the other. This small quarter, with a population of approximately 15,000 in its half-mile-square area, is 99 per cent Italian. There are almost no transients; indeed, most of the North End's problems today stem from overstability. Family relations are close, neighborhood ties strong, and there is virtually no ethnic intermingling with the rest of the city. Italians are a gregarious people, who love to be jammed together in their streets and houses as well as at dances, parties, and festivals—to the despair of the urban-renewal specialists, who think of any crowded area as a slum.

The great wave of Italian immigration reached Boston in the 1870s, some thirty or forty years after the Irish began to arrive. The Italians were too late on the scene, and too few, to compete with the Irish for control of the city's political machinery. Radical beliefs were strong, in the early years of this century, among Boston's working-class Italian immigrants; from this group came the anarchists Sacco and Vanzetti, whose crime and execution resulted in a *cause célèbre* for the American radical movement in the 1920s. Now the political coloration has shifted—as, perhaps, the balance of power is shifting. If the Irish run the city of Boston, the Italians, with their markets and produce-supply companies, can be said to feed it; and recently Italians have begun to make inroads on Irish political dominance throughout the state; in 1964 both the Republican and the Democratic candidates for Governor of Massachusetts were of Italian descent.

Most impressive of feast days in the North End is that of Saint Anthony, at the end of August, when a statue of this saint is borne in a great procession through the streets; ailing children are brought to kiss the saint, and money pours in from all sides to be pinned on the figure.

A political rally; Italian Americans support a countryman for Mayor of Boston.

Nearly forty years after their execution, Aldino Felicani *(opposite)*, anarchist and idealist, continues his efforts to vindicate the memory of his friends Nicola Sacco and Bartolomeo Vanzetti. Their case, which was waged through the Massachusetts courts for six years before they were finally electrocuted, focused dramatically the conflict not only between conservatism and the new radicalism but also between the old-line Yankees and the newly arrived immigrants. Mr. Felicani and a group of fellow believers regularly petition the Governor to reverse the decision of 1927 that sent Sacco and Vanzetti to their deaths. For these men the Sacco-Vanzetti case is not closed.

Death masks of Bartolomeo Vanzetti and Nicola Sacco

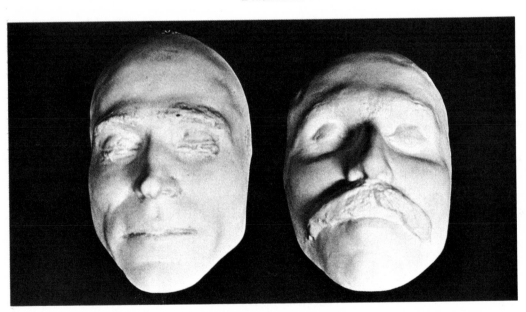

Faneuil Hall, with the Customs House Tower at left; its ground floor has been in continuous use as a market since it was built in 1742.

OPPOSITE: The Old State House, at the corner of State and Washington Streets; first erected in 1712, it was rebuilt, after a fire, in 1748.

OPPOSITE: The Bunker Hill monument, with three-decker Charlestown houses in the foreground

RIGHT: The Paul Revere House in the North End

BELOW: The Old Corner Book Store, at Washington and School Streets, built after the fire of 1711, now houses the *Boston Globe*.

Education

eed to know how to stop soil erosion in India? How to design a nose cone for a new type of missile? How to assess the rate of economic growth in the Soviet Union? Boston has few physical assets to distinguish it from other American cities of its size, but in its contribution to the nation's brainpower—its problem-solving capacity—the city can claim supremacy, through the specialized intellectual training offered by its numerous educational institutions.

There are some sixty colleges and universities in the Boston area, and the total of nearly 100,000 students attending them is rapidly increasing. Harvard University and the Massachusetts Institute of Technology, both in Cambridge, across the Charles River from the city, are perhaps the most renowned of these institutions; others include three women's colleges, Radcliffe—also in Cambridge and associated with Harvard—Wellesley, and Simmons; Boston College, in Chestnut Hill; Tufts University, in Medford; Brandeis University, in Waltham; and Boston University and Northeastern University, both in Boston. The city has been a leader in its public-school system as well; the Boston Public Latin School, established in 1635, was the first public school for boys in America.

HARVARD UNIVERSITY

Since its founding in 1636, Harvard's history has been closely interwoven with that of Boston. From a small local institution—the first graduating class, in 1642, numbered only nine—dedicated, as its 1650 charter put it, to "the advancement of all good literature, arts, and sciences," and "the education of the English and Indian youth . . . in knowledge and godlynes," Harvard has grown to a great national university; though it has retained its emphasis on liberal education, its 14,000 students no longer come exclusively from the ranks of the Boston and New England Yankee aristocracy (*so* exclusively, at one time, that between 1730 and 1790 no New Yorkers were enrolled in what was then Harvard College), but are qualified young men from every part of the world. Five Presidents of the United States have graduated from Harvard; and the list of distinguished alumni also includes leaders in business and in many of the professions.

The Harvard faculty, now numbering more than 5000, is a cosmopolitan group, including (of those pictured in the following pages) the Nobel Prize winners John Franklin Enders, of the Harvard Medical School, whose studies in virology helped in the development of the polio vaccine and later the isolation of the measles virus, and physicist Edward Mills Purcell, a member of the President's Science Advisory Committee, who has pioneered in the fields of nuclear magnetism and radiofrequency spectroscopy; the eminent classicist John Huston Finley, Jr., who is Eliot Professor of Greek Literature and has been Master of Eliot House for almost a quarter of a century; Paul A. Freund of the Harvard Law School, an authority on the history of the Supreme Court and on constitutional law; and the economist John Kenneth Galbraith, friend of and adviser to the late President Kennedy (a Harvard alumnus), whose career outside his Harvard professorship has included a stint as United States Ambassador to India.

Harvard's pre-eminence in certain specialized areas has been recognized in the form of a series of research contracts from the federal government, totaling over 30 million dollars a year, in science, medicine, public health, and other fields, which have brought not only money but able outsiders and new ways of thinking into the well-trodden and—some have said—overcultivated intellectual terrain around the Charles River Basin.

Sailboats on the Charles, passing MIT

OVERLEAF: Harvard Yard

Harvard and Radcliffe students in the library and *(above)* the *Lampoon* office

John Franklin Enders

John Kenneth Galbraith

Edward Mills Purcell

John Huston Finley, Jr.

82

Paul A. Freund

HARVARD COMMENCEMENT

Someone once called the Harvard Commencement the only true remaining American ritual. Far from being merely a magnificently staged graduation exercise, it is both a convention and a class day, and embodies much that both Harvard and Yankee Boston have traditionally stood for. No one can remember its ever having rained on Commencement Day, which is perhaps significant of the close relations said to exist between Harvard men and the powers on high.

The ceremonies begin with the arrival *(above)* of the Governor of Massachusetts in a horse-drawn carriage. Whether or not the Governor is a Harvard man, this tradition is never varied. A procession is formed, led by the Sheriff of Middlesex County, suitably costumed for the occasion, followed by the President of the University, the top-hatted Board of Overseers, and other dignitaries. The assembly is called to order by the Sheriff's striking the dais with the butt of his pikestaff. The graduating class then march to their seats, tipping their caps, as a voice admonishes them to do, to the statue of John Harvard.

Harvard Commencements in other days featured dissertations in Latin, Hebrew, and Greek, but today only the Latin dissertation is delivered, by a student *(opposite)* who addresses the assembly with suitable gestures in the best Roman oratorical style. After prayers, hymns, and an address in English, degrees are conferred on the graduating class by the President, the honorary degrees are awarded with further speeches, and a benediction is said.

The Commencement Day lunch that follows, of potato and chicken salad and beer, is a far cry from the magnificent collations that used to be served; but the afternoon parade of the alumni is a spectacle that over the years has changed only in its personnel. The oldest living graduate leads the procession; Frederic H. Curtis, of the Class of 1891, had that honor in the parade pictured on page 86. Following him through Harvard Yard were representatives of more than seventy years of Harvard graduating classes; some were too feeble to walk unaided, while others almost missed the procession in their eagerness to reminisce with classmates. And as the parade ended they parted, each firmly announcing that he had made his reservations for next year's Commencement gathering.

THE MASSACHUSETTS INSTITUTE OF TECHNOLOGY

MIT's contribution to the present-day economy of Boston, and its influence on the probable future of the area, have been enormous. From its classrooms and laboratories issues a stream of highly trained scientists and engineers to staff the numerous technological firms being established in and around Boston, particularly along Route 128. The facilities and brainpower of MIT have attracted large federal and private research contracts, and the school's presence in Cambridge is one major cause of Boston's being chosen as the site for the new NASA center for electronics research. And all this, of course, is to be seen in the context of scientific achievements and the advancement of technical knowledge in which MIT has pioneered in the more than one hundred years of its history.

Founded in 1861 by William Barton Rogers, himself a scientist and president of the National Academy of Science, the Institute first occupied a building on Boylston Street in downtown Boston. It began with fifteen students and seven teachers, including its founder, but has grown, since its move across the Charles River to Cambridge in 1916, to the proportions of a middle-sized American university, with 3500 undergraduates, 3000 graduate students, a faculty of 750, and a supporting teaching staff of 600. The MIT faculty is distinguished by the presence of scientists such as (of those pictured in the following pages) the late Swiss-born Hans Mueller, Jerrold R. Zacharias—both physicists—and Warren McCulloch, a neurophysiologist and mathematician who, with the late Norbert Wiener, helped to develop the field of cybernetics. Under the leadership of James R. Killian, Jr., president of the Institute for a decade, and of Julius A. Stratton, who succeeded him in 1959, the ideal of making MIT a university polarized around science has been advanced by the establishment of a School of Humanities and Social Science, and of the Sloan School of Management. Dr. Killian, now Chairman of the MIT Corporation, has brought the Institute into even greater national prominence through his service to the Eisenhower administration as the first Special Assistant to the President for Science and Technology and as Chairman, from 1957 to 1959, of the President's Science Advisory Committee.

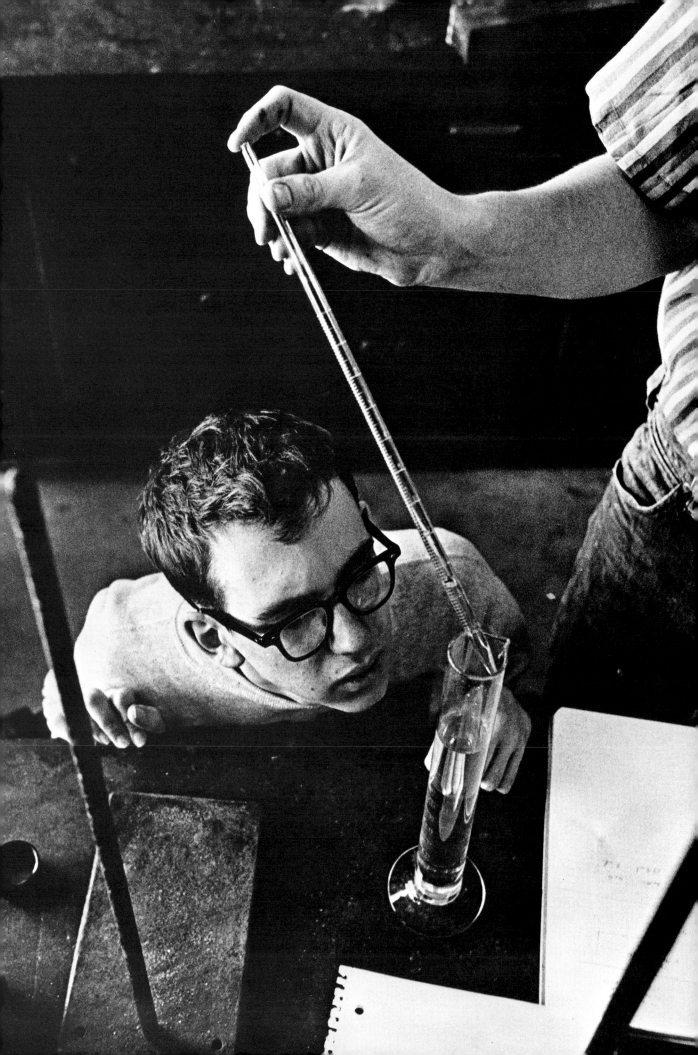

Students in the MIT laboratories

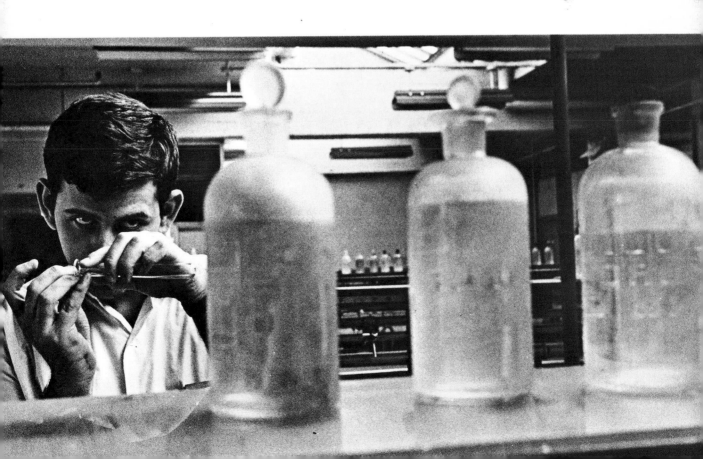

James R. Killian, Jr.

Warren McCulloch

Julius A. Stratton

Jerrold R. Zacharias

Hans Mueller

Route 128

An eighty-mile expressway around Boston, which links the city with the major highways of New England and New York State, Route 128 has become a byword in American business because of the many research and development ("R&D") firms that have located along it. Though its official name is the Greater Boston Circumferential Highway, it is commonly called the "space highway" because of the work done there on missiles and satellites by the many aerospace, electronics, and nuclear engineering companies. There are more than 350 technological firms located along the highway now, with an estimated annual payroll of over $400 million.

Often such firms were spun off directly from some MIT research project, as in the case of High Voltage Engineering, Inc., which was started when John Trump, chairman of the Electrical Engineering Department at MIT, became interested in the medical applications of a high-energy radiation machine developed originally for nuclear research by a colleague, Robert van de Graaff. In 1946 the two MIT faculty members joined with Denis Robinson of the University of Birmingham, England, in forming a company to produce the machine for the radiation treatment of cancer. Although the Van de Graaff machine is no longer used for cancer therapy, High Voltage Engineering, Inc., now produces about twenty-five of these machines a year for theoretical nuclear research, with a large percentage of the profits being plowed back into research and development.

Another Route 128 firm spun off from MIT is IKOR, Inc., founded by a group of MIT men headed by Arthur W. Winston, a Canadian, to do R&D work employing physics and electronic instrumentation. Mr. Winston and his associates in IKOR were until recently part of a larger concern known as Space Sciences, Inc., established in 1961, which had the responsibility for providing the measurements for the re-entry heat shield used in Project Apollo.

Boston brainpower is not all being put to R&D use. A young specialist in an older "think" firm, Arthur D. Little, Inc., founded in 1886 and located not on Route 128 but in Cambridge, is Jack L. Treynor, who hails from Iowa and attended both Harvard and MIT and whose field is finance. He has helped to develop a computerized method of projecting balance sheets and income statements to determine future earnings.

The Van de Graaff machine produced by High Voltage Engineering, Inc.

Arthur W. Winston

Medicine

ealth is Boston's third largest industry. Approximately 7000 patients are treated daily in 52 voluntary hospitals, many of them founded by first-family Yankees whose descendants still sit on the hospitals' boards.

The Harvard Medical School, founded in 1782 and for many years the only such school in the Commonwealth of Massachusetts, in 1870 became the scene of the greatest reform in medical education in the country when Harvard's President Charles W. Eliot insisted that the curriculum be made uniform and progressive in character, and that it cover three years (it was later extended to four), winter and summer. For the first time medical training was taken out of the hands of individual doctors, who had collected fees for awarding medical diplomas. The Harvard Medical School began to attract first-rate doctors, who came there to teach and to practice in Boston hospitals.

Boston's accomplishments in medical science itself, as well as in the teaching of it, are impressive. Dr. Oliver Wendell Holmes discovered and publicized the contagious nature of puerperal fever in 1843. Ether anesthesia was publicly demonstrated for the first time by W. T. G. Morton during an operation performed at the Massachusetts General Hospital in 1846 by Dr. John C. Warren. The separate efforts of three surgeons, Drs. William F. Bernhard and William E. Ladd of Children's Medical Center, and Dr. Robert E. Gross, resulted recently in the discovery of a new technique for performing cardiac surgery on "blue babies," previously considered inoperable. Dr. John Putnam Merrill of the Harvard Medical School, who is on the staff of the Peter Bent Brigham Hospital, has played a major role in research on kidney transplants and the development of the artificial kidney. And the city has several internationally known specialists, such as the cardiologist Dr. Paul Dudley White.

Dr. John H. Knowles, director of the Massachusetts General Hospital, believes that the tendency of local hospitals to affiliate with the great medical schools in the area (in addition to Harvard's, there are top medical schools at Tufts and at Boston University) has given Boston the best of two medical worlds: a combination of the latest research and the most highly trained practitioners with the best in patient care.

Not all the doctors trained in Boston stay there. Dr. Charles Alderson Janeway, physician in chief at Children's Medical Center and professor of pediatrics at Harvard

Dr. Charles Alderson Janeway

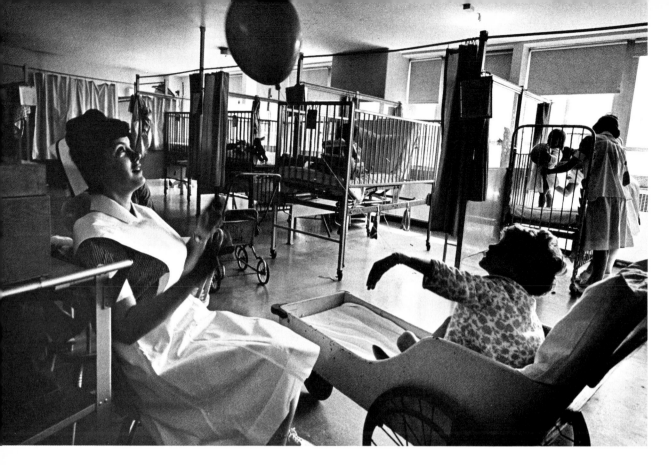

Medical School, is particularly proud of the foreign students he has helped to train; one of them, a Samoan, is today one of three doctors on his island; another, a Virgin Islander, has a practice comprising 24,000 children. The Children's Medical Center —one of eight hospitals directly connected with Harvard Medical School—where the photographs above, below, and opposite were taken, is one of the many reasons for Boston's continuing medical leadership.

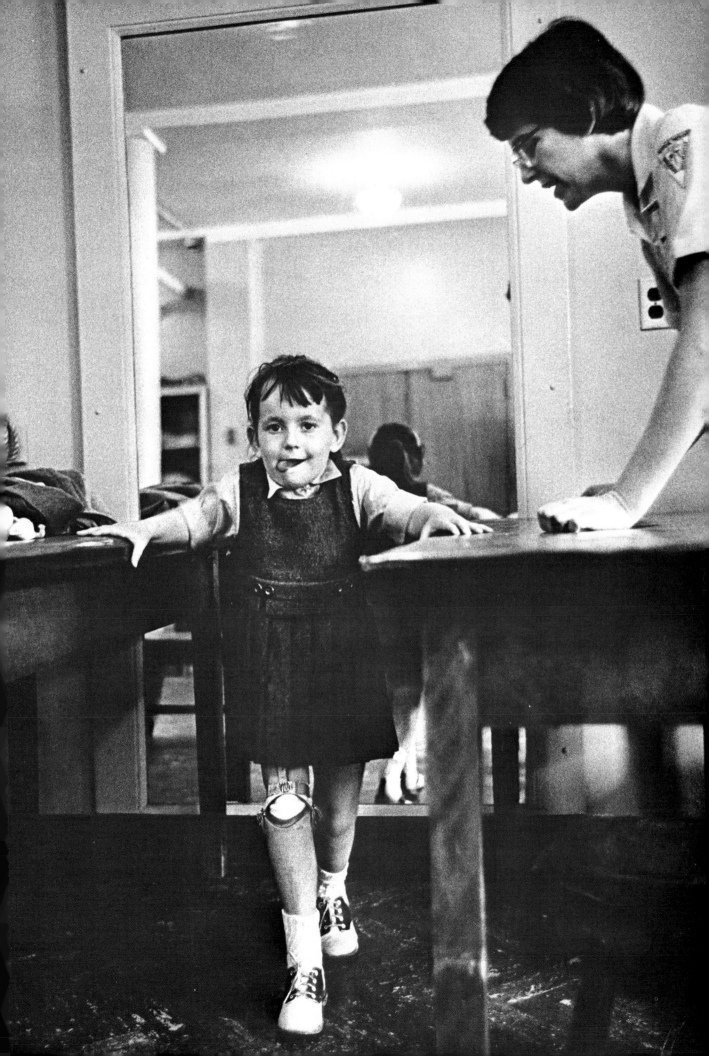

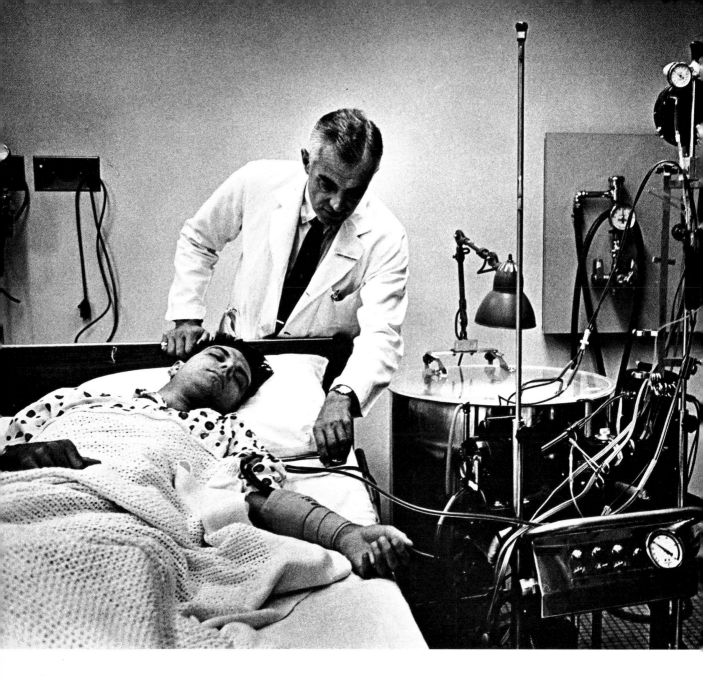

ABOVE: Dr. John Putnam Merrill, with an artificial kidney machine

Dr. John H. Knowles

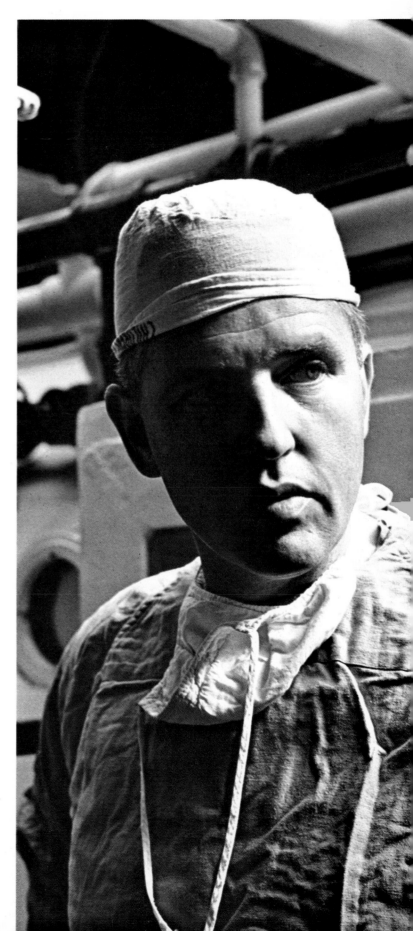

Dr. William F. Bernhard

III

The New Boston

Boston, the city that once boasted of being "the Hub of the Universe," was dying. Large areas had declined into slums. The harbor was almost completely inactive. There was hardly any new construction. The population decreased by over 100,000 between 1950 and 1960. Wealthy Yankee families fled to the suburbs, and prosperous businesses migrated elsewhere to escape the property tax, which had quadrupled in four decades. Meanwhile 42 per cent of the city's property was in the hands of educational institutions and museums, and thereby tax-exempt. Boston was facing bankruptcy.

When John F. Collins took over as Mayor in 1960 he pledged he would "get the city moving again." In his first term he pruned 1200 jobs from the city payroll, making it possible to lower the property tax from $101 to $96 per $1000. His attempts at reforming the city government earned him the respect of the Yankee banking and business community, and the Boston Citizens' Seminars at Boston College lent further impetus to a joint effort of Yankees and Irishmen to save the city. The alliance was recognized officially when in 1964 Mayor Collins became the first Irish Mayor of Boston to receive an honorary degree from Harvard.

One means of restoring the city's economic health is urban renewal. The program launched by Mayor Collins, under the auspices of the Boston Redevelopment Authority, may eventually expend over a billion dollars and will affect 25 per cent of the city's area and 50 per cent of its inhabitants. Heading the program is Edward J. Logue, a Philadelphia-born former labor lawyer who had already helped to make urban-renewal history in New Haven. "What kind of a country are we going to have if our cities are populated by people who want to get out?" asks Mr. Logue, whose enemies call him a "gray-flannel Irishman." "I have reason to believe we can stop that trend here in Boston. We hope to create a series of residential neighborhoods that will be in competition with the suburban neighborhoods for families. We want to better the schools and get rid of bad housing. And we hope to make downtown

(Continued on page 114)

Mayor John F. Collins receiving an honorary degree from Harvard, 1964

Edward J. Logue

The hole that was Scollay Square, and *(above)*
the model for the new Government Center

111

William J. Foley, Jr.

Charles A. Coolidge

Monsignor Francis Lally

(Continued from page 109)

Boston the most interesting place in the USA to work in, shop in, and walk around in. But we must be sure not to destroy the character of the city as it exists."

Among the projects under way is Government Center, a complex of modern buildings to occupy 60 acres in what was once Scollay Square, Boston's skid row area, that will house all the city, state, and federal offices formerly scattered over the city. Another is the Washington Park project in Roxbury, a Negro section of Boston. This project, now under the Boston Redevelopment Authority, was begun on the

Otto and Muriel Snowden

local level, largely through the efforts of an idealistic Negro couple, Otto and Muriel Snowden, who founded an organization called Freedom House to give Roxbury citizens a place to meet, talk, and mobilize for a self-help program to rehabilitate their neighborhood.

Belief in the "new Boston" has brought about some unusual partnerships. Working along with Irishmen Collins and Logue is the shrewd Yankee lawyer Charles A. Coolidge, product of Groton, Harvard, and Harvard Law School, who led bankers and businessmen to support redevelopment and is chairman of the Downtown Business District renewal committee. Another supporter of the program is

(Continued on page 120)

Roxbury citizens at a Freedom House meeting

OVERLEAF: Back Bay citizens protesting urban renewal at a City Hall meeting *(below)*

(Continued from page 114)

Monsignor Francis Lally, editor of *The Pilot,* the oldest Catholic news weekly in the country; Father Lally acts as a buffer between the city politicians, mostly Catholic, and the urban-renewal officials.

Collins and Logue do not have the support of City Council member William J. Foley, Jr. This outspoken opponent of the urban-renewal program regards it as just another means of victimizing the citizenry for the enrichment of real-estate speculators. There is opposition also from the citizens themselves: when Back Bay residents learned of plans to erect high-rise apartment buildings in the midst of the gracious early-nineteenth-century houses on Commonwealth Avenue, they immediately banded together to fight City Hall, and managed at least to stave off the new construction.

But progress—or anyway, change—is in the air. "The new Boston" is a concept rather than a fact, a feeling of hope rather than one of despair. Most of all, it is an expression of confidence in Boston's future as a great city.

THE BOSTON CITIZENS' SEMINARS

The new communication between Yankee banker and Irish politician owes much to what are now called the Boston Citizens' Seminars. A conference held in May 1954 at Boston College in Chestnut Hill, to bring prominent citizens of all backgrounds together to discuss Boston's problems proved such a success that it was extended into a series of seminars covering every aspect of urban living. The moving spirit behind the seminars is Father W. Seavey Joyce, Dean of the College of Business Administration at Boston College, who serves as president of a seventy-eight-member council that plans the discussions. Boston College, the third largest Catholic educational institution in the country, has, under its president, the Reverend Michael Patrick Walsh, S.J., proved an ideal place to hold the seminars. There, Yankee and Irishman can meet and talk; the lessening of tension between the two groups has been a prime factor in the advancement toward a "new Boston."

The Reverend W. Seavey Joyce

The Reverend Michael Patrick Walsh, S.J.

The 52-story Prudential Building, Boston's tallest

A wharf in the waterfront area

Sailboats on the Charles River

Carved wooden doorways in South Boston.

OVERLEAF: Boston Common in winter

The Irish

O f all the cities in America, Boston is the one most identified with the Irish, and South Boston, or "Southie," as it is affectionately called, is the Irish-American's spiritual home. It was Boston, the last stop on the Cunard steamship line, to which the immigrant Irish came, and where they rose from poverty and ignorance to run the city—as they do today. And it was South Boston to which most of them came to live—as they do today.

Desperately poor and often illiterate, like other immigrant groups, the Irish brought to America two large assets in addition to their willingness to work with pick and shovel: they spoke the language, as the other immigrant groups did not, and they had a solid background in politics. Oppressed and discriminated against at home in Ireland by the English and English law, to achieve any sort of justice the Irish had been forced to learn the uses of politics, and they eventually became highly disciplined and organized politicians.

Pouring into Boston, they found the American version of the hated English, the Yankee, owning and running the city. In South Boston the Yankees lived on the main streets, the Irish in the stables with the horses. For the Yankee, thrift, caution, and sobriety were socially desirable characteristics; the Irishman, sunk in poverty, found his escape in drink. In many Irish families the father died early from overwork or from drink; the widowed mother presided over the home life. Moreover, the Irish immigrants were Roman Catholics in what was then an overwhelmingly Protestant city. And, most important to the history of Boston, the Yankee thought of politics in terms of getting honest, efficient government at the lowest possible cost, while for the Irish politics was a means of providing necessities for their people and ultimately of redistributing the wealth.

Soon after their arrival, the Irish began building their political machine, block by block and neighborhood by neighborhood. The political boss, in all his various forms, became the most powerful figure in Irish South Boston. The first thing a newly elected Irish politician did was to expand city construction to provide work for the uneducated laborers among his people. When Yankee employers hung out signs saying: "Jobs available, Irish need not apply," Irish politicians got jobs for their friends and relatives as policemen, firemen, and schoolteachers. By 1900 the Irish population (Democratic) outnumbered the Yankee population (Republican) and the Irish political machine effectively controlled Boston.

Today's Boston Irish are mostly second- and third-generation American citizens. They are becoming dynasty conscious, in the Yankee tradition, and wealthy families such as the Kennedys now encourage their sons to enter public service and politics.

On Saint Patrick's Day, the wearin' o' the green prevails whether the politicians are Irish or not. *Left to right:* John Powers, Edward Brooke, Edward McCormack, Jr., Patrick ("Sonny") McDonough

The present-day Irish politician is a different breed from his forefathers. Young, well-educated, often armed with a law degree, sometimes even fortified with time spent in the Yankee stronghold of Harvard, he is sincerely interested in good government. President John Fitzgerald Kennedy was the finest flower of this development, was the

Speaker of the House John McCormack, and *(below)* his nephew, Edward McCormack, Jr.

A political meeting in South Boston

Roy Green of City Hall

embodiment of the Boston Irish American's dream. Almost every home in "Southie" displayed "Jack's" photograph, and there was pride in the knowledge that an Irish immigrant's grandson was in the White House. They even forgave him his Harvard association; he could do no wrong.

Another young Irishman in Boston politics, Edward McCormack, Jr., son of oldtime Boston politician "Knocko" McCormack and nephew of Speaker of the House of Representatives John McCormack, feels the glamour of a political career to be slightly lacking now. "Thirty years ago, Irishmen looked up to politics. Today, the Irishman looks down on politicians, thinking that they must be corrupt," he says. Mr. McCormack, formerly Massachusetts Attorney General, and unsuccessful contender for the Democratic Senatorial nomination won by Edward Kennedy in 1962, continues: "Oldtime elections depended on patronage. Today everything is civil service. They were ignorant then, and could be led—but now, with improved education, people think for themselves."

Mr. McCormack sums up the present position of Boston's Irish: "The Irish are no longer the abused minority, but the abusing majority." In "Southie" today there is a great deal of local pride in such sons as Richard Cardinal Cushing, and Father

Walsh, president of Boston College. There is only one Protestant church left. And the Irish cannot understand why the Yankee left the beautiful beach areas of South Boston for mosquito-infested Back Bay.

THE LEGEND OF MAYOR CURLEY

"The Yankee Republicans had the wealth and the power, but we Irish had the babies," explains Robert E. ("Roy") Green, a clerk at City Hall and former associate of the late Mayor James Michael Curley. "Politics is the major industry here. Like the Swiss, we live by our wits."

Mr. Green is only one of many in Boston who still owe their jobs to Curley, and to whom the very mention of the name brings a smile and a whisper: "He was the greatest." For most outsiders, Curley's name stands for political corruption, and he is remembered chiefly as the subject of a best-selling novel by Edwin O'Connor, *The Last Hurrah*. To Yankee Bostonians, Curley was the worst thief and scoundrel of all time. For Mr. Green and the Irish of his generation, he was their wonderful, brilliant leader. Whatever the point of view, Curley achieved the status of a legend in his own time. After his death, he lay in state for two days—an honor accorded to only three others in the history of the Commonwealth.

The facts of Curley's political career are simple: briefly, he was Mayor of Boston off and on for sixteen years, served four terms as a United States Congressman, one term as Governor, and two terms in jail. Mr. Green can reproduce Curley's own explanation of his first term in jail: "It was Thanksgiving and cold," Curley said. "T—— C——came to see me. He wasn't too well, and neither were his wife and three kids. I was twenty-two years old and just elected to the City Council. T—— said he was having a hard time making ends meet and asked me if I wouldn't go down and take the examination for letter carrier for him, since he wasn't educated enough to pass it himself. I thought to myself, Saint Peter won't hold it against me if I do T—— a small favor so that he can have bread and milk for his family. So I took the exam for him and finished first in the class. Some neighbor turned me in, and I had to take an enforced three-day vacation." Mr. Green is not too clear about the second "vacation" except that: "He was in Congress and slipping, and some fellows smarter than he put it over on him."

According to Mr. Green, Curley was a spellbinder. An appeal to sentiment was part of his basic campaign style. He never tired of telling of his poverty-stricken youth, of his widowed mother who scrubbed floors for a living. "I was born in a shabby tenement room in Roxbury, the worst slum in America," he used to say. "I lived in that room for eleven years and studied by candlelight as hard as Lincoln ever did. Then, at eleven, I got my first job to help out my mother. I came home with my first week's pay, a dollar and a half. It was December twenty-fourth, the day before Christmas. I was met by a man in a black suit who said, 'Jimmy, I'm the undertaker. Your mother passed on this morning.'" Mr. Green says he could go on like that for hours, after which the crowd cheered him and carried him around triumphantly on their shoulders. He was one of them.

Curley became a symbol to the immigrant slum Irish of their emergence from

The Irish, young and old, love to dance—especially the jig.
When there is a shortage of partners *(above)*, the girls look on.

nothingness to status in the political arena. Self-educated, he saw politics as the only road open to a poor Irishman, and he quickly came to power. At once he began to spend the taxpayers' money. He had promised more jobs, schools, playgrounds, parks, and beaches, and he delivered. Vast construction projects were started without regard to cost; if he ran out of money, he borrowed against future taxes. After all, it was the rich Yankees who would eventually pay those taxes. Upon the completion of his fourth term as Mayor he had accomplished two things: the face of Boston was almost completely altered, and the tax rate had quadrupled.

Curley's power began to wane as the Irish became more prosperous and better educated. Mr. Green describes a meeting between Curley and the young John F. Kennedy (whose maternal grandfather, John [Honey] Fitzgerald, Curley had defeated for Mayor), when the late President was an up-and-coming young politician. "I don't think they liked each other any. Curley did all the talking. Young John F. just sat there and smiled and smiled. He hardly said anything. Curley was passing out money as if it were going out of style. Young John F. just sat there—I don't think he had a dollar in his pocket. They were so different. It was another era. You could see that in a minute."

AN IRISH STORYTELLER

"I've lived in South Boston all my life, and I was twenty-seven years old before I met my first Republican," states Joe Madden, famed throughout Boston as an Irish storyteller.

Son of immigrant parents, Mr. Madden is head clerk in the Real Property Department in City Hall. He directs his wit primarily against the Republican Yankee, and especially enjoys telling stories about his fictitious "Aunt Delia" and "Uncle Dinny."

"My Uncle Dinny," he says, "went to the city of Boston election department the other day, and told the clerk he wanted to change his party designation to Republican. 'Why, Dinny,' exclaimed the clerk, 'you've been a Democrat for many years.' 'I know that,' explained Dinny, 'but I had a fight with my family and I want to do something to disgrace them.'"

An Uncle Dinny maxim: "When you see a politician walking instead of riding, you can be pretty sure he's thinking of running."

And an Aunt Delia story: "My Aunt Delia worked as a young greenhorn [a term used for people just over from the old country] for a family on Beacon Hill. The lady for whom she worked was staging a dinner in her palatial residence. The evening of the affair, she said to Aunt Delia, 'Delia, I want you to stand at the door of the ballroom and call the guests' names.' 'Good,' answered Delia. 'I've been waiting to do that for five years.'"

Joe Madden of City Hall

136

SAINT PATRICK'S DAY IN SOUTH BOSTON

Saint Patrick's day in "Southie" means much more than merely painting the white line down the middle of the street green for the parade. It is a very special occasion, on which the forces of nature seem to cooperate with man to make a uniquely Irish masque.

March 17 dawns with clear skies and the cheerful voice of the weather reporter predicting a mild and sunny day—just perfect for a parade. This is nonsense. Everyone knows that there will be rain and snow and freezing cold by the time the parade starts. No one can ever remember good weather for the parade—or a prediction of bad weather by the forecaster. Nobody minds.

By noon, children have already gathered by Dorgan's restaurant to watch the city's politicians arrive for the traditional corned-beef-and-cabbage lunch. This is a special gathering, for it is a bi-partisan group, and it meets not to make decisions but to bend the elbow, break bread, and tell jokes. The spirit is that of a college reunion, only here the alumni are past and present holders of political office, a little silly and gay, coming back to "Southie" to reminisce.

Amid the clanging of silverware and the tinkling of glasses, Senator Leverett Saltonstall rises to make a spech. He is loved here, for although he is as blue-blooded a Yankee as can be found in Boston, he has, according to no less an authority than the late Mayor James Michael Curley, an Irish face. "Ladies and gentlemen," begins "Salty," as he is affectionately known, "I am very happy to be in Southie, and today I consider myself an Irishman." "Salty," interrupts Johnny Powers, Clerk of the Supreme Court of Massachusetts, "if there's any Irish blood in you, it must be on your chauffeur's side." And so the words continue until it is time for the main event—the parade.

By now the temperature is down to freezing, and a brisk snowstorm is in progress. As the parade moves along its four-mile route, the contrast between the smiling and waving politicians and the thoroughly chilled and wet spectators, too uncomfortable to wave their banners, becomes increasingly sharp. But the political smiles never waver, and the parade-watchers stoically endure until the very end. It is tradition.

The crowning event of the day is the appearance of the junior Senator from Massachusetts, Edward M. (Teddy) Kennedy. Senator Kennedy marches through South Boston evoking all the passions and aspirations of the Boston Irish. Each must touch the tall, husky young man with the flashing smile as he makes his triumphant way through the ranks of his people.

As the last marchers approach the reviewing stand, there is the traditional sharp break in the weather as the sun comes out and the temperature rises. The spectators go home, but the politicians now begin a round of parties. Democrat and Republican, victor and vanquished, arm in arm, they will be singing "When Irish Eyes Are Smiling" all through the night.

Senator Edward M. Kennedy makes his triumphal appearance

Governor John Volpe

Senator Leverett Saltonstall

BELOW: Former Governor Endicott Peabody, with
Clerk of the State Supreme Court John Powers

NOVEMBER 22, 1963

All over the city, Bostonians received the news of President Kennedy's assassination with shocked faces and unconcealed grief

The harsh nasal voice and the tall, gaunt figure of Richard Cardinal Cushing played a memorable part, for the whole world, in the funeral service for President Kennedy. But in Boston the ubiquitous Cardinal has long been a familiar and beloved sight.

Born in South Boston of an immigrant father, he graduated from Boston College and seriously considered a political career before turning to the Church. It is not surprising that he shares the political acumen and wit of the many colorful figures who came out of the same environment. Involved in everything going on in Boston, Cardinal Cushing is not shy about expressing an opinion on any subject, from urban renewal to his activities on the board of the City Hospital. As an outstanding liberal, the Cardinal has backed many of the reforms now being put into effect in the Roman Catholic Church. His humorous stories, often at his own expense, are famous and often repeated throughout the city.

Index